Portrait of a Seaside Town

Portrait of a Seaside Town

Historic Photographs of WHITSTABLE

From the

Douglas West

Collection

First Printed December 1984
Second Edition February 1985
Third Edition December 1987

Paperback ISBN 0 9508564 4 4
Hardback ISBN 0 9508564 5 2

Text set in Baskerville 11pt

Printed and Published in Great Britain by
Emprint Publications, 9 Harbour Street, Whitstable, Kent CT5 1AG

This reproduction of J. Andrews' map of 1807 shows mainly the Turnpike road to Canterbury dotted with milestones (shown in the centre of the road) and numbered 3, 4, 5, 6. Also plainly shown is the Burnan which rises in Blean Wood and flows to the sea at Swalecliffe. It is now, of course, widely known as Swalecliffe Brook. The Turnpike road ends at Whitstable Street and there is no direct road to Swalecliffe and Herne Bay.

ACKNOWLEDGEMENTS

Mr. Wallace Harvey for his enthusiasm, for everything historical to do with Whitstable, for his vast knowledge of the history of Whitstable and its people, but above all for his invaluable help and assistance. Many of the facts in this book are due to his tremendous amount of knowledge.

The "Whitstable Times and Tankerton Press".

Miss Margery Feaver for her skill and help in producing these photographs.

The Whitstable people, who have loaned and given me old historic photographs of Whitstable and without whose help and kindness this collection would not have been possible.

BIBLIOGRAPHY

Cox's Guide to Whitstable 1884.

"Chestfield" *by Wallace Harvey 1975.*

Story of Seasalter Churches *British Publishing Co.*

The Canterbury and Whitstable Railway *I. Maxted.*

Bell Book and Boys *Whitstable Boys School.*

The "Whitstable Times and Tankerton Press".

Succourest! – this was thy work
This was thy life upon earth.

Mathew Arnold

WHITSTABLE

"Ther abowt they dragg for oysters" so Leyland informs us in the XVth century. Oysters have been dredged here from the earliest recorded times and, until quite recently, was an important part of the industry of Whitstable. Indeed, a century ago more than a hundred oyster boats were to be seen off shore. It is obvious that this number of vessels needed sails, rigging, repairs, but above all a crew of several men to operate each one, and when there were but about three thousand inhabitants here these constituted a considerable portion of the population. At the beginning of the 19th century the construction of the harbour and the railway to Canterbury brought further opportunities for trade and industry. Large quantities of coal were brought by colliers from Newcastle to be unloaded and transported by railway. Even Stephenson's "Invicta" locomotive was brought here by sea from Newcastle. At this time the Whitstable shore was lined with shipyards and an important aspect of transport was the operation of the Whitstable Hoy, when Thames barges, that maid of all works, operated a transport facility around the coast, unloading their cargo on to horse-drawn carts at the aptly named Horsebridge. Over 7,000 of these vessels were built altogether – only a handful remain today.

This then was the picture of Whitstable covered in the photographs which follow, photographs that begin only a couple of decades after photography was invented by Fox Talbot in England and Louis Jacques Mandé Daguerre in France. Years before the motor car, years even before the bicycle came to emancipate women, there was a camera man in Whitstable, a town of one policeman, one doctor and one postman.

This collection of photographs and their description is not intended to be a complete history of Whitstable, but only a photographic recording of that history encompassing a hundred years, but it is a fascinating story.

Douglas West

Portrait of a Seaside Town

Not exactly an ideal shopping centre. Pavements, formed about 1860, are as bad as the roadway. Nothing faster than horse-drawn traffic clip-clopped its way along what was then called "Whitstable Street". "Whitstable" was the name given to the Church Street and All Saints Church area. The cottages and steps on the left are now occupied by the Salvation Army Citadel which was opened in December 1886. Barclays Bank now occupies the site of Fenn the clockmaker. Fenn's was taken over by Mr. Holden the jeweller and Mr. Hollebon the watchmaker could be seen at work in the window. The centre of the photograph, which was taken about 1860, shows where Spenceley's the drapers were and which was later to become Ricemans, then Dawsons and now a row of smaller shops. Surmans the butchers at No. 57 and 59 were next door to the Maypole Dairy Co. and next door to that was Mr. Butcher the baker – still a bakers today. Gladstone Road had not yet been opened. On the left of the photograph Church and Co. occupied the premises next to Bonners Alley, much later to become the Picture House Cinema and now of course the Fine Fare Supermarket. Church and Co. later moved across the road and were eventually taken over by Mr. Arthur Collar ironmongers and builders merchants. Messrs. Boots Chemists now occupy these premises. The gap between the two buildings (4th and 5th from the right) shows the entrance to Youngs Cottages, a row of wooden cottages stretching towards Regent Street, all now demolished. The new Post Office in Gladstone Road now occupies this site.

This photograph taken some years later from a similar standpoint shows that Gladstone Road has been opened, the Salvation Army Citadel has been built and a few more shops opened.

High Street

The "Queens Head" inn was right in the centre of the High Street – it is now a bookshop (Pirie & Cavender). This photograph was probably taken about 1910 when there were many parades and processions that everyone turned out to watch. Shown here is the naval cadet Fife and Drum band marching in company with crowds of schoolboys. The shop to the right of the "Queens Head" at this time was a confectioners but is now a hairdressers, and next to that is the entrance to the Endowed School which at this time taught boys as well as girls in separate halves of the school.

Taken about 1900 this photograph shows the Whitstable Pharmacy No. 39 High Street. The proprietor Mr. Knight was a photographer as well as a pharmaceutical chemist as quite a number of his photographs have been found. Most chemists about this time were the only people who would process amateur films and plates as a knowledge of chemistry was essential. The "Whitstable Times" office next door was established in 1863 and has been in the Cox family ever since: Mr. William Cox, the proprietor, published a number of Whitstable guides as well as selling stationery and best Morning China Tea at three shillings a pound! The tall building on the extreme left of the photograph was Ambrose Bonners drapers shop. The alley here is still named Bonners Alley after him. There are a number of these alleys from the High Street through to Middle Wall and Island Wall and these were a quick and easy way through to the sea. This building later became the International Tea Stores.

High Street

This photograph is of the Congregational Church in the High Street which was erected in 1808. The small shop on the right is Mr. Fred Gann's builders and undertakers shop which was demolished in 1920 when the church was enlarged, the centre doorway and steps discontinued and an entrance built at the side. The church has recently been sold and transferred to the Hall in Middle Wall. The old church is now the "Playhouse" Theatre.

This photograph is interesting for the view of the four cottages Nos. 103 to 109 High Street, now, of course, a row of shops (Herberts Cycle shop and the Whitstable Stationers). The "Ship Centurion" Inn is seen in its original guise before the front was rebuilt. Skinners clothing stores (now Griffeys) is shown next to Skinners Alley, the pathway to King Edward Street. The photograph was taken from the Congregational Church where guests can be seen leaving after what seems to be a wedding as it is attracting the interest of bystanders. It is certainly taken on a weekday as the shops are open.

High Street

This view of the High Street photographed from the "Duke of Cumberland" Hotel demonstrates the unhurried traffic that was typical at the turn of the century. Hatchards clothing shop on the left now occupies the site of the "Lower Hope" public house. A little farther down the street were the "Shades" and the "Hoy Endeavour". The "Shades" inn was one of the oldest in the town. No. 13 High Street, now Courts furnishing store, is the site of the old "Hoy Endeavour" a public house associated with the old smuggling days. The original "Prince of Wales" was a low building which was pulled down in 1898 and originally called the "Jolly Sailor", now the Job Centre. On the other side of the High Street the "Royal Naval Reserve" also had a new name. For many years it was known as "The Rose", but in 1867 was changed to its present name in honour of the Royal Naval Reserve who had distinguished themselves in the recent war. On the extreme right of the photograph which was taken c. 1890 is a photographic studio and next door is a barbers shop complete with the usual striped red and white pole. In 1854 a general furnishing shop was established next to it and farther down the street is the Gunston Commercial Hotel and Dining Rooms, and out in the roadway there's a quiet, leisurely pace to everyday life. The shops on the left of the photograph were known as 'Cheapside'.

The old "Prince of Wales" public house which lay back from the High Street. It was a very old inn dating back to the 17th century and originally named the "Jolly Sailor". This was changed to the "Prince of Wales" to commemorate the wedding of the Prince of Wales in 1863, later to become King Edward VII. The inn was associated with smuggling activities and was demolished in 1898 when Messrs. Flint and Co. built the modern "Prince of Wales" which too has now closed and the site is now occupied by the Job Centre.

High Street

Prince of Wales Public House, High Street

Whitstable Harbour Station

This is the only known photograph of a passenger train in the original railway station. Taken c. 1890 it shows three carriages with their distinctive lamp containers. The porter walked along the carriage roof and inserted the lighted lamps before the train started. The station was located inside the eastern harbour gates and the line crossed Harbour Street with a level crossing. A new station was built on the south side of Harbour Street in 1894 but when passenger traffic ceased in 1930 this was then closed. The Whitstable Health Centre now occupies the site of this 1894 station. At the turn of the century the original station became derelict and that too has now been demolished.

Taken about the same time (1890) this photograph shows in more detail the ticket office and waiting room at the old harbour station – the stationmaster standing on the line is Mr. W. London. The view on the extreme left of the photograph shows empty fields as Tankerton had not started development at this time. A signal box and gatehouse was built on the south side of the level crossing.

The last train

The last train to leave Whitstable Harbour was on 29th November 1952 when locomotive 31010 went on its way to Canterbury. On the left is a corner of the original station. The disastrous flood of 1st February 1953 which destroyed part of the main line over the Graveney marshes necessitated opening the railway line again on the 5th February whilst repairs to the main line were made. On 28th February 1953 the line finally closed and the track dismantled.

One of the oldest photographs of Whitstable – the junction of Oxford Street and Canterbury Road was taken c. 1858 and shows the the toll gatehouse almost in the centre of the photograph. Built in 1737 it was demolished c. 1860 to make way for the bridge to carry the railway over Oxford Street, and it was rebuilt at the bottom of Borstal Hill. The wooden bridge was drawn across the road in August 1860, a temporary station having been built at Kitchenham Place (now Clifton Road). The gas lamp by the white gate, now the opening to Belmont Road, was one of the first in Whitstable, being erected in 1850. The toll was abolished when the turnpike road was freed in 1871.

Another photograph taken in 1904 from a similar standpoint shows the wooden bridge, the station and the newly erected Adelphi Terrace. The "Railway Inn" has scarcely altered. Mr. Rollingtons Railway Shaving Saloon is shown by the group of three children. He was a keen photographer and may well have taken the photograph. The photograph also shows the station cab rank on a blind corner which graphically illustrates the pace of traffic before the advent of the motor car.

Canterbury Road

The old forge on the extreme right of this photograph was built in the late 1700s when Mr. Pettman was the blacksmith. It is sited right opposite the "Two Brewers" in Canterbury Road. On the extreme left is an old 'clapper gate' which gave access to a footpath which crossed the railway to West Cliff. The photograph was taken in the late 1890s.

The tollgate at the bottom of Borstal Hill was built c. 1860 when the tollgate at Oxford Street was demolished to make way for the railway station and the bridge across the roadway. The horse trough was given by Arthur and Myra Pinero in 1896. Arthur Pinero the famous dramatist and playwright was knighted in 1909. The horse trough was replaced with another one in 1936 by the Metropolitan Drinking Fountain and Cattle Trough Association.

Canterbury Road

Joy Lane

Manor House

The Vicarage, Canterbury Road

Built for Thomas Gann (1801–1870), the Manor House near the Irish Village, so called because of the Irish names to the houses, is a vivid illustration of the 'Good Old Days', sadly, alas, no more. The house is now a block of flats and, when this photograph was taken, close by was a sports field which was the venue for cricket and football matches.

The vicarage in Canterbury Road, the home of the Reverend Henry Maugham and where, as a child, his nephew Somerset Maugham stayed after the death of his parents. The vicarage was later to become the home of Doctor Nesfield and when he left the house was demolished and the area built over.

The Bear & Key Hotel

Picture House Cinema, High Street

A rare early photograph showing two entrances to the "Bear and Key" Hotel which was established in 1703. Flowers in pots decorate the window ledges. A window was later substituted for the doorway on the left. Early oil paintings of the inn sign depicting the bear and a key now hang in the Castle. There are extensive stables and coach-houses at the rear of the hotel where the horses were kept for the Norwich Union fire engine which was given to Whitstable in 1866.

Originally a furniture store belonging to Church and Co. the "Picture House" was built in 1913 and during the next few years Mr. Paton, the manager, and his wife, the pianist, showed the old silent films which are now in film archives. In the 1920s he also was a keen builder of wireless sets and received the broadcast 2LO from London which he amplified in his cinema. Entrance to the cinema was down the side of the building (shown on the right of the photograph) as the screen was immediately behind the front wall of the cinema. A very unusual 'ticket' was issued from the semi-circle office in front of the cinema. This took the form of a cut out brass blank. Rebuilt and renamed the "Argosy" it was seriously flooded during the great flood of February 1953. Later redecorated and renamed the "Regal" and opened by Miss Joan Dowling it finally closed in 1960. Shortly afterwards it was completely rebuilt once more to become the Fine Fare Supermarket.

Tankerton Green was the end of the road when this photograph was taken c. 1880 because Tower Gardens Road, Tankerton Road and Northwood Road had not been opened. Tankerton Green is still recognisable today as the semi-circular lawn and shrubbery at the end of Tower Parade. At this time there was a deep well in the centre of the Green – it can be seen partially obscured by the man standing on the pathway. Tower Parade had not yet been started. On the extreme left of the photograph is the Wynn Ellis Almshouses, previously Pearsons Hotel which was built c. 1828. It was purchased in 1874 by the Lord of the Manor Wynn Ellis and converted into almshouses in memory of his wife who had died some years earlier. To enable Tower Gardens Road to be constructed the gateway to the Tankerton Tower had to be set back and this was done in 1896. Since this photograph was taken the pathway along this stretch of Harbour Street has been raised and railings fitted. The first house in Tower Parade was built in 1890 when the Tankerton Estate was formed.

Photographed in the 1880s this is the original weatherboarded "Steam Packet Inn". Tower Parade had not yet been started. On the extreme right of the photograph open fields can be seen, where now, of course, Tankerton and Northwood Roads are built. The "Steam Packet" in the photograph was burnt down in October 1913 and later rebuilt in conventional brickwork.

Tower Parade

Harbour Street

This is a very early photograph c. 1870 of the south quay of the harbour showing the rounded tops of the railway trucks. The weatherboard building on the left is the original customs house. In the distance are the two tall chimneys of the coke ovens, used for making coke for the early locomotives. These were built in 1847 and demolished in 1892, the bricks being used for foundations of Tankerton Road, one of the first roads to be made by the newly formed Tankerton Estate Co.

This photograph of harbour personnel c. 1950 shows in the background the "Great Eastern" public house on Ludgate Hill and opposite the harbour gates. The personnel are, left to right: W. C. Bennett, retired Station Master; F. C. L. Cann, Harbour Master and Station Master; C. Wills, carter; F. Sponder; E. Gambrill; Jack Wills, a past Harbour Master; J. W. Parker, retired Harbour Master. The harbour at this time was owned by British Rail and in January 1958 was sold and handed over to the Whitstable Urban Disctrict Council. Horses were used to deliver railway goods around the town and often used for hauling railway trucks in the harbour.

The Harbour

Harbour Railway Personnel

Mr. W. Pettman, nicknamed 'Billy Plum Bun', a baker in Harbour Street, used to tour the streets selling rolls and cakes often ringing a bell. He had a large head for such a tiny man. This photograph was taken c. 1910 in Gladstone Road.

The Whitstable Town Beadle and Town Crier, Mr. Dixon, in his uniform with 'Old George', Mr. George Fisk landlord of the "Railway Tavern", Harbour Street (now "The Punch") who was an indefatigable collector for charities in the 1920s.

This photograph of the start of the Whitstable to Herne Bay Walking Race was taken c. 1903. It started from the Cross (marked by a lamp post in the roadway outside the Duke of Cumberland Hotel) to the Herne Bay Clock Tower and back. Tankerton had not then been made up so the competitors had to go via Old Bridge Road and South Street to Herne Bay Road.

Terrys Lane which runs from Middle Wall to the High Street was made up by Mr. Goldfinch in 1900 with wide granite kerbs which have now been covered with tarmac. The large house on the left has now been demolished, and a ticket office of the East Kent Road Car Co. on the corner was destroyed by a bomb on 13th August 1940.

Whitstable—Herne Bay Walking Race

Terrys Lane

This photograph shows the girls' section of the Board School in Oxford Street taken c. 1892. The school was opened on 8th October 1877 by the Rev. W. Blizzard, Chairman of the Board. Mr. Kirkby was the headmaster here for about 40 years. The schoolteacher in the centre of the photograph is Miss L. Carlton, daughter of the licensee of the "Foresters Arms" in Albert Street. Carlton Terrace in Northwood Road was named after her by the builder Mr. Edgerton in 1892.

There were a number of private schools about this time in Oxford Street, Nelson Road and Canterbury Road. Mr. and Mrs. John Wood had a school, Daylesford House High School, in the 1880s and Miss Selby was the head of Cecil House School in Oxford Street. The Misses Dyer were the principals at the Springfield House School in Canterbury Road at this time. The Whitstable Institute was established in 1864 and a few years later was located in the Assembly Rooms on Horsebridge Road. A visit to the reading room there cost just one penny. As late as the 1930s Mr. Sanders had a private Collegiate School in Shaftesbury Road and Miss Soderberg was the principal of the Argyle School at 9 Nelson Road. This photograph is thought to be the Daylesford House School.

The Board School Oxford Street

A Whitstable School

The "Coach and Horses" public house – originally two cottages – is shown towards the centre of this photograph which was taken c. 1905 and before its modernisation. The photograph is interesting as it shows the old Whitstable Urban District Council Offices which were later to be demolished to make way for the public library. The council offices were then transferred to the newly purchased Tankerton Tower and renamed the Castle. Between the "Coach and Horses" and the council offices is the entrance to the Board School which was built by Mr. Cephas Foad in 1876. Down this small roadway can be seen the first gas lamp to be erected in the town, fixed to the rear of the pub. In the roadway can be seen a performing bear tethered to his keeper by a chain and a long pole. These itinerant performers could be seen round the neighbouring towns and villages. The drapers shop lit outside by three large gas lamps was owned at this time by Mrs. Alice Maxted, was the Faversham Co-op until 1932, and in 1933 was rebuilt by Mr. Field as a furniture store. The houses on the corner of Nelson Road on the extreme left of the photograph have all been converted into shops. After the First World War the War Memorial was sited behind the wooden fence and the small trees in the centre of the photograph.

Nos. 24 and 26 Oxford Street photographed c. 1880. The oriel window is still to be seen between this building and the S.E. Electricity Showrooms next door. The group of small children who appear to be in uniform in front of the house seem to suggest it could be one of the small private schools that were in Whitstable at this time.

Oxford Street

Photographed about 1900 these pictures show cargo being unloaded onto horse-drawn carts to be taken over the Horsebridge which was kerbed and paved, and still to be seen, although the centre is now breaking up. Several thousand Thames barges had been built, flat bottomed, and they would settle on the hard flat beach where they could be unloaded at low tide. The Whitstable Hoy at this time made three trips a week from London and the Horsebridge was constantly in use.

The Horsebridge

Horsebridge Road

Whitstable Oyster Company's Stores

This is an early photograph of The Cross and Horsebridge Road. On the left is Ansdell House, the home of Dr. Salt and in the 1920s of Mr. A. Wood who established his garage there. The Cross was marked by a gas lamp post in the centre of the road in front of the Duke of Cumberland Hotel. Further along the road is the Assembly Rooms Theatre and the unusual store shown in another photograph. In the centre background is the headquarters of the Whitstable Oyster Co.

The headquarters of the Whitstable Oyster Fishery Co's premises on the Horsebridge. The Royal Appointment was granted in 1894 and the sign 'Royal Native Oyster Stores' placed over the Royal Coat of Arms. The Freemen of Whitstable, as the fishermen were called, were answerable to the Crown and not to the Lord of the Manor. A Thames barge can be seen on the 'Hard' for unloading by horse and cart by the Horsebridge. On the extreme right two public houses on Sea Wall can be seen. The weatherboarded building next to the Whitstable Oyster Stores is the "Dredgermans Arms" and the taller building next to that is the "Stag", now a private house. The free fishers of Whitstable were governed by 'an Act of Parliament Incorporating the Company of Free Fishers and Dredgers of Whitstable in the County of Kent and for the better ordering and government of the Fishery' which was dated 30th April 1793.

Harbour Street and Sea Street

After the Great Fire of November 1869

On the right of this photograph which was taken about 1910 is the old "Victoria Inn" and is today the premises of the Whitstable Yacht Club. The roadway has been widened and the path has been built up and railings fitted. Along Harbour Street among the shops was the "Spread Eagle" Inn, where the church of the Harbour Street Christian Fellowship now stands. The "Spread Eagle" was in the area of the great fire which occurred on 10th November 1869 when 71 buildings were destroyed. The castellated building in the centre, "Harbour Buildings", was erected in 1905.

A portrait of Queen Victoria can still be seen scratched on the surface of one of the windows in the Whitstable Yacht Club. It is remarkable that this link with the old pub has survived for more than a hundred years. The artist is unknown.

The great fire of Harbour Street occurred on Monday 10th November 1869 when 71 buildings were destroyed. This photograph taken a few days after the fire shows the devastation each side of Sea Wall and the Copperas Road, now Sea Street. In the 18th century the area was known as the Old House Field. Gone are the houses on Sea Wall together with the "Victoria" pub. In the centre of the photograph is Ludgate Hill but today dominated by Harbour Buildings, a castellated building erected in 1905.

Tankerton Pier nicknamed 'The Bedstead' was sited opposite Pier Pavilion now part of the Royal Hotel. It was constructed in 1894 and opened on 2nd August of that year. It was 112 feet long and 15 feet wide. A wide road was constructed from Marine Parade to Bennells Avenue and named Station Road as at that time it was hoped to construct a railway station at Ham Shades Lane but it never came to fruition so the road was renamed Pier Avenue. It was hoped that this road would be the main shopping area of Tankerton, but the construction of the Marine Hotel, George Fitts Garage and the Post Office near Tankerton Circus formed the nucleus of the shopping area of Tankerton. The Tankerton Pier fell into disuse and was finally dismantled by Mr. George Warner in 1913.

The earliest photograph of Tankerton Slopes taken c. 1900 showing the Tankerton Estate staked out with name boards along Tankerton Road which, until the early 1920s was an unmade road from Tankerton Circus onwards. Marine Parade was unmade and what is now the Marine Hotel (but at that time Cliff Terrace) was built in the 1890s by Messrs. Gann and Co. of Teynham Road. The end house was a convalescent home and later converted to a hospital during the 1914–1918 war. It was the forerunner of the Whitstable and Tankerton Cottage Hospital. At this time the whole of Tankerton Slopes were offered free to the Whitstable Urban District Council but the offer was refused. Some time later the council paid £750 for them. The slopes were the northern boundary of St. Annes Farm until taken over by the Tankerton Estate Co. in 1890. St. Annes Farm was demolished in 1930.

Tankerton Pier

Marine Parade

A very early photograph of Tankerton Beach taken about 1880 showing the tea booths in the foreground with Mr. Angel, complete with top hat, who opened the first tea booth here. In the background can be seen the beginning of the Beach Road Arcade with buildings right out on the beach. The gate to Beach Road can also be seen. Swings have been here since very early times and have only recently disappeared. The two tall chimneys of the coke ovens in the harbour which were built in 1846 to supply coke for the early railway engines were demolished in 1892.

This photograph which was taken about 1895 shows Tankerton Beach with numerous people enjoying the fine weather. In the background is the Clock House (the tall building on the beach), behind it the row of tea booths famous for its shrimp teas etc., and on the right a number of bathing cabins. It will be noticed that quite a number of ladies are protected with umbrellas – sun bathing was, apparently, not very popular. The Clock House was destroyed by fire in 1915.

Tankerton Beach

This is an early photograph of the Seasalter and Ham Oyster Fishing Co's premises and also of the capstan on the beach (silhouetted against the white wall and near the two men carrying sacks of oysters). In the background is a veritable forest of masts and rigging of the colliers in the harbour. Over the top of the Oyster Co's building is the chimney of the engine house, later to become the harbour light, and on the beach the flagstaff – both of which have now disappeared.

Tankerton Beach

Tankerton Beach and East Quay

Tower Parade

Tankerton Beach

A later photograph of Tower Parade. At this time c. 1893 only four houses had been built here. It will be noticed that the front entrance was reached by a flight of steps and the path had not then been raised to the level that it is today. A few houses appear to be built on Tankerton Road but the large house on the extreme right of the photograph is Nos. 3 and 5 Northwood Road which was the home of Dr. Parris Piper, a local doctor for 28 years when he came here in 1902.

The tea booths on Tankerton Beach were a very popular venue for people coming from Canterbury by the railway. Shown here are Angels, Kemps and Butlers tea rooms about 1880. On the extreme left is one of the bathing cabins first seen here in the late 18th century. In the foreground is an early three-wheeled push-chair, very much like a bath-chair.

Tea Booths, Tankerton Beach

The Bandstand, Tankerton

The tea booths, which were such an attraction at the end of the nineteenth century for the visitors from Canterbury and, of course, the people of Whitstable, were established on Tankerton Beach from 1856 onwards by Angels, Kemps and Butlers. People were brought here from Canterbury for a shilling on the Canterbury and Whitstable Railway, popularly nick-named the 'Crab and Winkle' line because the lure of sea food was so great. The booths shown in this photograph were the last to survive in this way. A more modern row of tea booths was built nearer to the harbour and in one of these – Mr. Offredi's – was the venue for the formation of the Kent Yacht Club in 1905. In the following year the name was changed to the Whitstable Yacht Club, now internationally famous with their own premises on Sea Wall which was originally the "Victoria" public house.

The Bandstand was a popular feature on Tankerton Slopes, especially on Regatta Day. The Thames barge dressed overall was the starting point for yacht races etc. Regattas have been held here since 1792 except for the war years. Most years a firework display ended the days entertainment. Various Whitstable bands performed in the Bandstand which was built before the First World War by Mr. Porter to the design of Mr. George Reeves, but it has now long since disappeared.

Marine Terrace after the great storm and flood of 29th November 1897. Workmen are seen clearing the houses of the vast amount of beach and mud washed up onto the gardens and in the lower rooms. The "Old Neptune" has been completely destroyed and the wooden buildings at the rear are at a crazy angle, but the two wooden cottages almost on to the beach seem to be standing with little damage. The end house of Marine Terrace with the bay windows is the original office of the Seasalter & Ham Oyster Fishery Co.

A typical photograph of the fishermen's huts and stores which were built all along this part of the beach, showing outside steps to the upper part of the stores. A Thames barge lies off the Horsebridge. During the years these stores suffered severe damage from storms and floods.

Marine Terrace

Fisherman's Stores

The original "Old Neptune" public house on the West Beach destroyed in the great flood and storm of 29th November 1897. This photograph was taken about 1880 and the proprietor then was Henry Keam and is the only known photograph of the front of the building. Originally a boat-building workshop it was later converted to a public house. Mr. Keam died in 1895 and was spared witnessing the destruction of his property. His son carried on the business after his father's death but lost all his property and possessions a couple of years later in the great storm. After the flood the two cottages on the west side of the site were rebuilt as the "Old Neptune".

This photograph is of the Coastguard Station on West Beach. The site was marked by a flagstaff and a lockup hut on the beach in front of the main building, and was manned by the Royal Naval Reserve. Bathing cabins can be seen on the beach. All this has now gone and the coastguards in Whitstable are represented by a mobile unit. Behind the building now are hard tennis courts.

The original Old Neptune

Whitstable Coastguards, West Beach

An early photograph of the Fife and Drum Band marching through the High Street about 1903 when they were known as the Wesleyan Sunday School Band. Later they were known as the Whitstable Lads Naval Brigade and today as the Whitstable Sea Cadet Corps. Bonners Alley (next to the International Stores) is the Headquarters of the unit today. They were commanded by Lieut. Magnus Teeling, a member of the Royal Naval Reserve and Chief Officer of the Seasalter Coastguard Station.

The Whitstable Sea Cadet Corps is the oldest Sea Cadet unit in the country, formed in 1854 as the Wesleyan Sunday School Band. This photograph was taken soon after World War II and they are seen marching at almost the same spot as the photograph above. This well disciplined unit is always in evidence at carnivals and other, more serious, occasions.

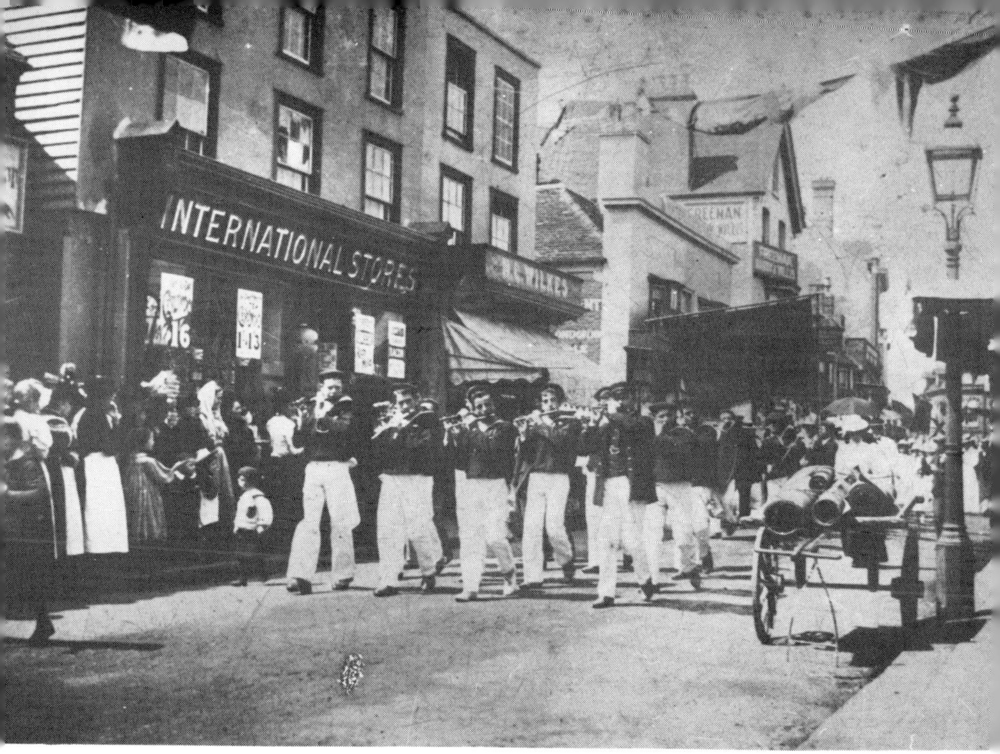

Fife and Drum Band

Whitstable Cadet Corps

The Shipyards

Marine Terrace

Sollys shipyard and slipway is typical of the shoreline of Whitstable in the 19th century. The photograph shows three Thames barges (the nearest one without masts) taken c. 1900. All along the beach too were fishermen's huts and stores. The "Old Neptune" public house can be seen in the distance, rebuilt after being destroyed in the 1897 storm.

A very early photograph showing part of Marine Terrace and the rear of the original "Old Neptune" inn which was destroyed in the great storm of 1897. The front of the inn is obscured by the two white weatherboarded cottages. A stain down the side of the old pub shows where the beer dregs were emptied out of the window.

The extremely busy interior of the Seasalter and Ham Oyster Fishery Co's premises on the Harbour. Sorting, grading and packing the oysters in tubs and barrels went on right through the winter months ending in April.

A consignment of oysters on the old Whitstable railway station. The platform of wood reached right across the bridge, also made of wood, over Oxford Street. Oysters were sent all over the country and to main shipping lines. Most were packed in barrels but some were packed in straw baskets. The platform was reached by wooden steps. At this time oysters were about seven shillings a hundred.

Seasalter & Ham Oyster Fishing Company

Oxford Street Railway Station

Typical Whitstable fishermen of the 1890s returning with nets full of oysters. Knee high leather boots would be worn and occasionally a bowler hat was to be seen.

When the oyster fleet was at work, four or five men would be used to dredge and haul the oysters on board to be sorted from shells, starfish, stones, etc. The dredge was made of iron rod with a net fastened to a wooden bar across the bottom.

Oyster Fishermen

Dredging Oysters

This photograph of the Whitstable Oyster Fleet taken c. 1900 shows the numerous oyster boats that were to be seen off Whitstable. Over a hundred were working at the turn of the century. This photograph was probably taken during a race on the occasion of the regatta. There were two companies of oyster dredgers, the Whitstable Oyster Fishery Co. based on the Horsebridge and the Seasalter and Ham Oyster Fishery Co. with premises on the East Quay of the Harbour.

Another photograph showing the sorting and grading of oysters at the Seasalter and Ham Oyster Fishery Co's premises on the Harbour.

Oyster Fleet

Sorting Oysters

Dan Sherrin

Electioneering, Harbour Street

Mr. Dan Sherrin with his "Seasalter Fire Brigade". He endeavoured to run his own Seasalter Carnival. He was an eccentric character but a gifted artist. This photograph was taken about 1930.

Electioneering in the early 1900s. Mr. R. T. Lang, a Liberal candidate, addressing a crowd in Harbour Street outside the "Railway Tavern" (now "The Punch"). The whole road would be blocked with people – it was little hindrance to the small amount of traffic as there was always a route round the back streets. This whole area was dubbed 'Starvation Point' as no one ever seemed to flourish there.

The Frozen Sea 1895

The Frozen Sea 1929

The sea at Whitstable has frozen over from time immemorial because of the amount of river water entering the sea at the estuary of the Medway. This is the first recorded photograph of a frozen sea taken in February 1895. It was to be another 34 years before the next one, here photographed on 15th February 1929. This was followed by the sea freezing in 1938, 1940, 1947, 1956, 1958 and 1963. During the frost of 1895 there was great poverty in the town. A relief committee was organised and £200 distributed to the needy as well as soup, bread and coal. Mr. George Reeves gave dinners to 80 children each day at his bakery at 72 High Street, next to the old Post Office.

Taken from the Oxford Street end of Nelson Road this photograph of the flood of 29th November 1897 shows vividly the height of the water in this part of Whitstable. One can see the dark water-line on the bricks of the houses the length of Nelson Road, reaching the centre sash of the windows. The house being constructed on the left is now a dental surgery. A hundred years earlier this whole area was covered by the sea.

The great flood of 1st February 1953 is seen here in the High Street on the following morning when the water reached about three feet. This photograph shows the Salvation Army Citadel on the left and Barclays Bank on the right. The Lord Mayor of London Sir Rupert de la Bere visited Whitstable to inspect the damage.

The Flood of 1897

The Flood of 1953

Another eccentric Whitstable character was Mr. Dan Sherrin who lived in Joy Lane. He was a talented landscape artist and on occasions would trade his pictures for goods. He was a gifted artist too in woodwork. The photograph is interesting as it shows the original stand at the Whitstable Football Club at Belmont. Mr. Sherrin is shown preparing to kick off at a charity match.

The Rag and Bone Man is not seen these days, these were the last people to cry their wares in the street. For rags, bones and jam jars a few coppers were exchanged, and for children a brightly coloured windmill on a stick was the reward. Touring the streets with the cry 'Rags, bottles or bones' different men would have their own peculiar way of crying for their wares. The photograph shows children receiving their small reward.

On the extreme left of this photograph is the "Brewery Tap" public house – the oldest house in this part of Oxford Street. When it was built it was on the shoreline as the tide came up to the edge of Oxford Street. The "Brewery Tap" was associated with the early smugglers as a tunnel was discovered some years later under the road connecting cellars on each side of Oxford Street. In 1913 Mr. Breach, a motor engineer, took over the premises and altered the building into a garage which was novel in those early days of the motor car. He also generated a 110V electric supply to the confectioners across the road. When this photograph was taken c. 1890 there were no shops on the right until one became Arrowsmith the Chemists (now Cheadles). The light plaster fronted building with the three long first floor windows and the small front garden has been built up and is now the Tele Radio Co. A map of 1768 shows only the two cottages on the extreme right, later pulled down to build Stroud's bakers and E. Camburn, tailor.

The lower photograph shows Mr. Breach's garage Nos. 20 and 22 Oxford Street, the site of the old "Brewery Tap" inn.

Oxford Street

F. J. Breach's Garage, Oxford Street

Opening the Parish Hall

Hartsfield Terrace, Oxford Street

The Clergy from St. Alphege Church at the ceremony of opening the new Parish Hall on April 25th 1906. Tea was provided in the Parish Hall afterwards. The stage was decorated with plants, tables on the stage and on the main floor were adorned with spring flowers. All sorts of chairs were used – even long wooden bench seats.

Hartsfield Terrace is a row of cottages between Cromwell Road and Canterbury Road. Built in 1848 the end three cottages on the extreme right of the photograph were dismantled twelve years later and rebuilt brick by brick across the cul de sac in Swanfield Road to make way for the railway station and the wooden bridge which was drawn across Oxford Street in 1861 to carry the railway on its way to Ramsgate. Cromwell Road had not been opened at this time (it was opened in 1892). This photograph was taken about 1858 and is one of the earliest taken of Whitstable.

Jack o' the Green

Carnival Entry

Jack o' the Green dancers in the High Street in connection with the Whitstable Fair. Photographed outside the Congregational Church before it was enlarged. Tragically, soon after this photograph was taken the man's paper costume caught fire and he died from his injuries. Photographed c. 1910.

One of the earliest photographs of the Whitstable Carnival depicting an oyster shell with the pearl in the person of Eva Tilley on a two-wheeled truck garlanded with flowers and the Whitstable Urban District Council badge (hardly discernable in the old photograph). It was made to the design of Mr. H. Wilman, a furniture dealer in the High Street.

The visit of Queen Mary on 15th September 1915 to Barn House, Joy Lane, the coronation gift of the Mary's of the Empire who subscribed to the fund. Barn House was a convalescent home for working girls and in the First World War was a convalescent hospital for the war wounded. The Vauxhall car was driven by Miss Dot Carson who drove the Queen from the newly built railway station to Barn House and back. During the visit the Queen walked to the beach to inspect a bathing hut provided by her for the girls. She was accompanied by Lady Bertha Dawkins.

This is Barn House in 1912 when it was a convalescent home for working girls. Originally the home of Mr. George Reeves it was converted to a convalescent home for the war wounded. Barn House was built in the 15th century and contains a remarkable king post truss in the roof. Queen Mary visited the home on 15th September 1915 being driven from the railway station by Miss Dot Carson.

Queen Mary at Barn House

Barn House

Whitstable Urban District Council

Ambulance Brigade

The Whitstable Urban District Council photographed in the Council Chamber at the Castle. Councillor G. J. Johnson, J.P. was Chairman from 1948 to 1951. The Council has now been absorbed by the Canterbury City Council along with Herne Bay. Standing: L. M. Thomas, G. Vickery, W. C. Harvey, T. H. W. Foreman, F. Tomlinson (Treasurer), P. D. Donovan (Town Warden), W. K. Morris (Town Clerk), G. S. Dunkin (Surveyor), G. P. Young (Deputy Clerk), G. T. Snashall, F. W. I. Whitehouse (Sanitary Inspector), F. T. S. Chant, E. W. Cooper.
Seated: G. H. G. Foreman, J. Barton, H. Johnston, D. R. Cheadle, W. J. King, G. J. Johnson, J.P. (Chairman), C. Edkins, Col. A. A. Hawkes, C. M. Robinson, J. P. Prangnell, F. V. Fitt.

This unusual building, on the Horsebridge Road, was situated next to the old Assembly Rooms Theatre. It was a store with an ancient ship's figurehead at the top of the weatherboard building. The figurehead is that of the 'Chance' which is still in existence. The building was demolished to enable the Assembly Rooms to be enlarged some years later. The Assembly Rooms were opened in February 1868.

The British Red Cross and St. John Ambulance Association photographed c. 1920 with their first motor ambulance.

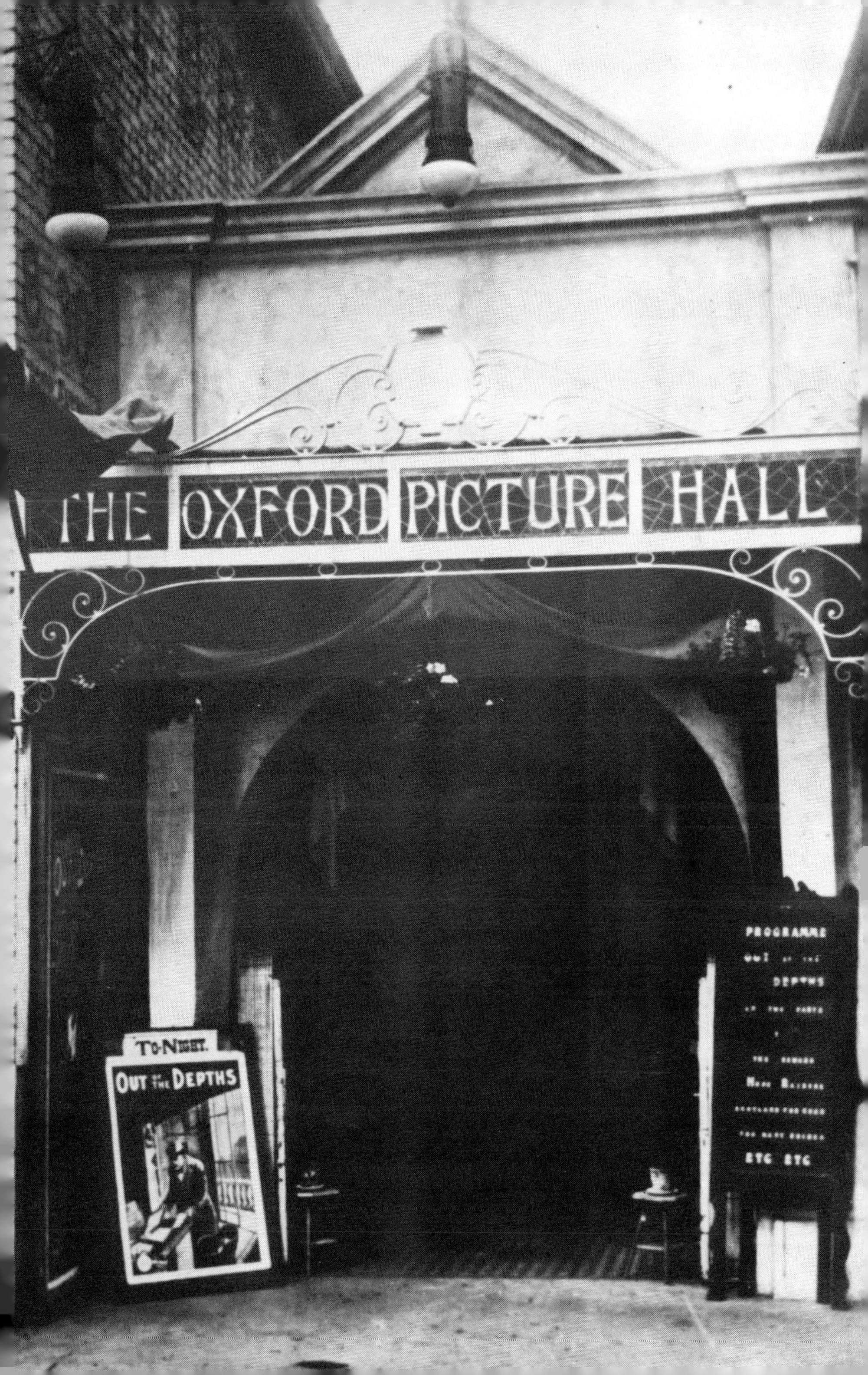

THE OXFORD PICTURE HALL
TO-NIGHT.
OUT OF THE DEPTHS
PROGRAMME
DEPTHS
ETC ETC

This is the first photograph ever taken of the new Norwich Union Fire Engine given to the town c. 1867. It was taken in the yard of the "Bear and Key" hotel where the horses were kept in the stables there. The manual fire engine was housed in the Fire Station in the High Street which was part of Mr. Tom Rigden's corn chandlers premises. In the event of a fire the ostler, on hearing the maroon fired by Mr. Rigden, would trot out two horses down to the fire station where they would be harnessed to the engine. Firemen, who were employed all over Whitstable, would then have arrived at the station, mounted the engine and off they would gallop to the fire to the excitement of a crowd of onlookers. A fire alarm bell can still be seen on the side of the shop (now Hedges). Firemen in the photograph include W. Brannan, T. G. Browning, – Coleman, R. Uden (Sen.), W. Gammon, – Browning (Jnr.), R. Uden (Jnr.), W. Wyver.

The original Oxford Picture Hall. This cinema started showing films in 1912 and was still a cinema more than seven decades later. The building shown in the photograph was demolished in 1935 and completely rebuilt and enlarged. The outside was constructed first and the old building taken down inside – all within six weeks. The new building has 800 seats. Mr. Wally Dukes has been the chief projectionist since 1936. Altogether four cinemas have been built in Whitstable. As well as the Oxford there was the Picture House in the High Street, the Palais de Luxe in Harbour Street and the Trocadero on Marine Parade. The Oxford ceased showing films in October 1984.

A later photograph showing the manual fire engine in use at a farm. Water was often used from ponds. This appliance was last used in the late 1920s when it was replaced with a Merryweather motor appliance and the fire station moved from the High Street to the Horsebridge Road in 1930.

Fire Brigade

Fire Brigade

This is the Merryweather motor fire appliance which replaced the old Norwich Union manual engine. Named the 'Native' it had solid tyres and chain drive and was in use up to World War II. The driver was for many years Mr. Tom Rigden, the proprietor of the corn and seed shop next to the High Street fire station. The firemen in the photograph are left to right: Mr. Harman (standing in road), Bill Richards, Edgerton Moyes, Charlie Hurlock, 'Cracker' Smith, Wellesly Poole, 'Doody' Blyth. Driver Tom Rigden, Second Officer George Fisher, Captain 'Weasel' Rigden.

A charcoal burner in Clowes Wood. This ancient craft often handed down from father to son was responsible for large areas of forest to be destroyed in the iron age. It is not known how much this process was used in our local woods. The photograph was taken c.1950.

The old railway bridge over Church Road (now Old Bridge Road). It was constructed in 1826–1830 to carry the Whitstable–Canterbury railway line. The old bridge was finally demolished in 1969 and the road widened. It was the oldest railway bridge in the world. Tankerton Halt, constructed and opened in July 1914, was nearby.

This is the earliest known photograph of St. Alphege Church in the High Street which was erected in 1845 and consecrated by the Archbishop of Canterbury on 9th October 1845, the first stone having been laid by Sir William Bridges, Bart. in August 1844. The cost was £4,000. Alterations to the interior were made in 1876 and the West Gallery was added in 1862. The photograph shows the church was lit by gas burners. This church was meant to replace the old Seasalter church, the registers of which date from 1558. The lower photograph shows the church decorated by two large murals.

St. Alphege Church

Seasalter Old Church is dedicated to St. Alphege and consists only of the chancel which dates back to the 12th century. A nave was added in 1616 but was pulled down in 1846. Alphege, Archbishop of Canterbury, was murdered by the Danes at Greenwich in 1011. He was buried in St. Pauls. In 1023 the relics were conveyed to Canterbury to be re-interred in the Cathedral. They were carried by road as far as Rochester and thence by sea and near Seasalter the party landed for a three day rest and Alphege's bones were housed in Seasalter church. In recognition of this honour the church was re-dedicated to St. Alphege. It was previously dedicated to St. Peter. This original church was destroyed by the sea in 1099. A storm in 1799 uncovered the foundations off the shore of this ancient church.

The parish of St. Peter was formed in 1935 from the parish of All Saints. A temporary building in Sydenham Street was erected in 1902 and in 1925 the present church was completed. A part of the temporary building is now used as the Scouts Hall in Acton Road.

Old Seasalter Church

St. Peters Church

The dedication of St. Andrews Church in Grimshill Road by the Archbishop of Canterbury, Geoffrey Fisher, on 26th September 1955. In the centre are the Rev. John Gore and Canon Waynforth.

The original Hamilton Road Mission was erected in 1931 from an army hut. It has now been completely rebuilt.

Dedication of St. Andrews Church

Hamilton Road Mission

A rare and unusual photograph of the Castle grounds when dancing and other entertainments were organised after the Second World War. The area has now been developed into formal gardens.

Tankerton Tower (The Castle)

Thatched Cottage, Swalecliffe

The Rectory, Swalecliffe

The post office in Swalecliffe seems to change place quite frequently. The photograph shows it to be located in a part of old thatched cottages, opposite what is now Swalecliffe Court Drive and next to the Old Forge on the south side of Herne Bay Road. In the early 1900s, the post office was in a cottage fronted by a lily decked garden and next door but one to the old "Fan" public house, opposite to what is now Elmwood Close. In yet another move the post office was opened in the modern Broadway next to the Hardware Stores. It is now a fish shop. Its fourth move and present position is opposite the garage and service station.

The Rectory, Swalecliffe, photographed in the early 1920s and recently demolished to make way for the modern Community Centre.

Swalecliffe Church

The Maypole, Swalecliffe

The Church of St. John the Baptist, Swalecliffe, was built in 1875 in place of a much earlier one, the registers dating from 1558. Some years later the top of the wooden and tiled steeple was blown down. The photograph also shows the old Swalecliffe Court Farm with Swalecliffe Brook in the foreground. The farm buildings have now all been demolished and the area built over; it now comprises a council estate.

Dancing round the maypole in Swalecliffe in the early part of this century to celebrate the coming of May and garlanded with flowers and long coloured ribbons which were plaited and unplaited by the dancers as they gyrated around the pole. The prettiest girl in the village was crowned 'Queen of the May'. Strange as it may seem, it was the chimney sweeps holiday as well.

The Chestfield Bowling Green was located on the east side of Chestfield Road before the road was widened and straightened, and opposite Silk's nurseries. The area is now a leisure playground. This photograph taken in the 1920s includes Mr. George Reeves who was, at that time, developing Chestfield.

An early photograph of the Chestfield Tennis Club taken in the late 1920s. The courts and pavilion were on ground now occupied by Nos. 105 and 107 Chestfield Road.

Chestfield Bowling Club

Chestfield Tennis Club

The "Stag" inn on Sea Wall. This photograph taken at the rear of the inn shows a weatherboarded structure with large windows which look right out over the sea and is dated about the 1890s. The "Stag" inn (now Stag Cottage) was near the Whitstable Oyster Co's store on the Horsebridge. The building shown in the photograph has changed very little today.

A very old 1863 photograph of the old "Guinea Inn" in Island Wall. W. H. Pettman in his top hat stands in the doorway. He established the inn in 1861. It is reputed to be the only inn so named in the country – because large profits were made by smuggling guineas to France. In recent years it has been altered and enlarged.

GUINEA
INN

Another view of the harbour showing colliers lined up stem to stern. The engine house and its chimney with its black top and the little steam crane can be seen in the centre of the picture competing with the 'jumps' a wooden structure of five steps from which two men would jump off backwards to 'jump' baskets of coal onto the railway trucks.

Crowded with shipping, the harbour at the end of the 19th century was a focal point of the town. Colliers from the north of England brought coal to the south for transport by rail. The Whitstable Hoy Co. was busy too carrying all kinds of cargo around the coast by Thames barges, seen here in the foreground. In the background can be seen the colliers which transported the coal.

The Harbour

This device known as the 'jumps' was a wooden structure of five steps on which two men 'jumped' coal from the colliers on to the rail trucks. Men in the hold would load coal into baskets which were then hooked to ropes from spars on the mainmast, then the two men on the quay would jump off the

'jumping horse' backward, hauling on the ropes to lift the coal to the deck, a process which would be repeated to lift the coal to the railway truck. This method of unloading coal was last used in 1928. During the 1870s men were paid 1½ pence per ton for this arduous work.

This photograph of All Saints Church was taken about 1870 before the restoration in 1875 and shows only three windows on the south wall. The ancient church tower which was restored a year or two earlier has six bells cast in 1729 from three earlier bells. The west wall and the north west corner of the aisle were rebuilt in 1873. The church dates from the 15th century and the registers date from 1556.

An early photograph of All Saints Church taken after the restoration which was completed in 1875 by Mr. Cornelius a local builder and shows the new mausoleum which Mr. Wynn Ellis had built and in which he and Mrs. Wynn Ellis now rest. The churchyard was closed in 1857 when the cemetery at Millstrood was established, but a gift of land by Mr. Wynn Ellis in 1874 reopened the churchyard.

All Saints Church before the Restoration

All Saints Church

An early photograph of the forge in Church Street and the "Monument" inn. The forge was later converted into a furniture shop for Mr. Kirby and was,later still,demolished to form an entrance to the car park for All Saints church and church hall.

Smeeds Farm as it was in the 19th century showing the original thatched barns etc. In 1824 a part of the area adjoining Smeeds Farm, known then as Barnfield, was sold for the coming Whitstable to Canterbury railway. The farm was then occupied by Thomas Richards. Mr. Beer was the owner in 1847 when it was known as Church Street Farm. James Smeed, who was the owner in 1863, gave his name to the farm but after a few years took over the Temperance Hotel 'Waverley House' at 15 Harbour Place which was later to become a 'home for young ladies'. In recent years Waverley House has been a fish shop and, sign of the times, a Chinese take-away. The tall building, Ivy House, in the background of this photograph which was taken about 1900, has now been demolished and the area developed and named Ivy House Road.

The Forge, Church Street

Smeeds Farm

Feakins Mill built c. 1785 in Church Road (now Belmont Road) was a three storied smock mill and the first miller there was Leonard Laws until 1836 when Robert Feakins took over and gave his name to the mill. He was followed by John Alfred Johnson until 1894. It was demolished eleven years later. A steam engine was installed in 1868. Commercial offices have been built on the mill foundations.

Borstal Hill Mill

Feakins Mill

Borstal Mill, built at the end of the 18th century, was a landmark of the Trinity House until 1885 when it was tarred. Sir Henry Irving purchased the mill in 1904 and converted the interior to a studio. He entertained many of the leading actors and actresses here. He was followed by his son Laurence. These photographs (see also page 124) appear to be the only ones showing the mill to be painted white – its original colour – and actually working. The Mill House was erected about the same time as the mill.

The octagonal tower was built with some of the material from the demolished house which stood by the south east corner of the bowling green. It is the oldest part of the present building. The photograph shows the North Lodge in the far centre which has now been demolished and the area made into a small car park.

Mill House, Borstal Hill

Tankerton Tower

A Sunday schools' procession in the early 1900s en route to a field for the annual 'treat' which was the highlight in a childs year. Interesting too is the stretch of the High Street which changed tremendously in the years to follow. The photograph was taken from the old Post Office looking towards the Duke of Cumberland Hotel. Surmans the butcher (No. 57) is on the extreme right. Spenceleys the drapers is the shop with the four large gas lamps in the front and a barbers shop in between. Surmans completely rebuilt the front of their premises in 1928.

Mr. Wynn Ellis, Lord of the Manor, was born in 1790 in Northamptonshire. At 22 he was a successful cloth merchant, was a Member of Parliament for 18 years and a magistrate of Kent and Hertfordshire. He moved to Whitstable to Tankerton Tower. He erected the Wynn Ellis Almshouses in 1874 in memory of his wife who had died some years before. He died in 1875 and is buried in the mausoleum which he had specially built in All Saints Churchyard. He owned a valuable art collection.

This photograph shows a procession in the High Street in celebration of the relief of this frontier town in the South African War. Defended by Col. R. S. S. Baden-Powell it was relieved by Col. Mahon and Col. Plumer after a five months siege by the Boer forces on May 17th 1900.

High Street

afeking Day at Whitstable, May 19th, 190

Chestfield Golf Club House is reputed to be the oldest club house in the country. Originally an old Dower House it dates from the 14th century and consists of cottages of Balsar Street Farm. It was bought by Mr. George Reeves who purchased 700 acres of land at Chestfield with the intention of building a Tudor style village and golf club with the course stretching over Shrub Hill. Mr. Billmeir then purchased the land from the executors of the late George Reeves and it is now wholly owned by the Chestfield Golf Club.

The inauguration of the Chestfield Golf Club in 1924 photographed in front of the Old Barn at Chestfield, a building that dates back to the 14th century and the site of Balsar Street Farm.

Golf Club House, Chestfield

Opening Chestfield Golf Club

This aerial view of Chestfield was taken c. 1925 before Chestfield Road was widened and straightened. In the foreground can be seen the old 14th century barn and the Chestfield Golf Club House and the north and south oast houses. Chestfield village dates back a thousand years and consisted then of only a few houses and four farms. In the 1920s Mr. George Reeves built a Tudor style village, many of the oak timbers coming from Hales Place, Canterbury, a monastery that was demolished.

The Manor House at Chestfield dates back at least to the 13th century. In 1346 a member of the family James Chestevill paid the Feudal Aid to knight the Black Prince. The building is situated at the corner of The Drive and The Drove and opposite Chestfield Farm, one of the four farms that constitute Chestfield Estate, the other three being Balsar Street Farm, Highgate Farm and Bodkin Farm.

Chestfield

Chestfield Manor House

The Wheatsheaf, Swalecliffe

Swalecliffe Coastguard Station

This photograph shows the old "Wheatsheaf" inn right on the roadway. Farther down the road is the old post office and the "Fan" public house. The old "Wheatsheaf" is now demolished and built way back from the road – a modern building with a car park in front.

The original old coastguard station at Swalecliffe which was later replaced by a row of terraced cottages and built on a new site further east. The coastguards are now a mobile unit in the town.

Call-up of the Royal Naval Reserve in 1914 photographed outside the "Railway Inn" and the old railway station showing the construction of the original wooden bridge over Oxford Street. Note the iron pillars supporting the ends of the bridge. This bridge was drawn across Oxford Street in 1861. It was replaced by the present steel bridge after the new station was built. The old station building is now a club. The boy in the Norfolk suit, second from the right, is our well known historian Wallace Harvey.

Whitstable divers were renowned for their skill and dived on many important wrecks. On the left is Harry Gale, in the centre Fred Rigden and – Bartlett on the right.

Goal Running was a popular sport in Whitstable during the early part of this century. Clubs were formed in neighbouring towns, notably in Faversham. This photograph shows the Whitstable club in 1902/3 and was in existence in the 1920s. The club won a number of silver cups. The game is basically a game of 'tag'. The runners would try to run round a distance mark and back without being 'caught'. A 'starter' would send the runners on their way.

The Whitstable Football Club – the Thanet League Champions 1908/9.

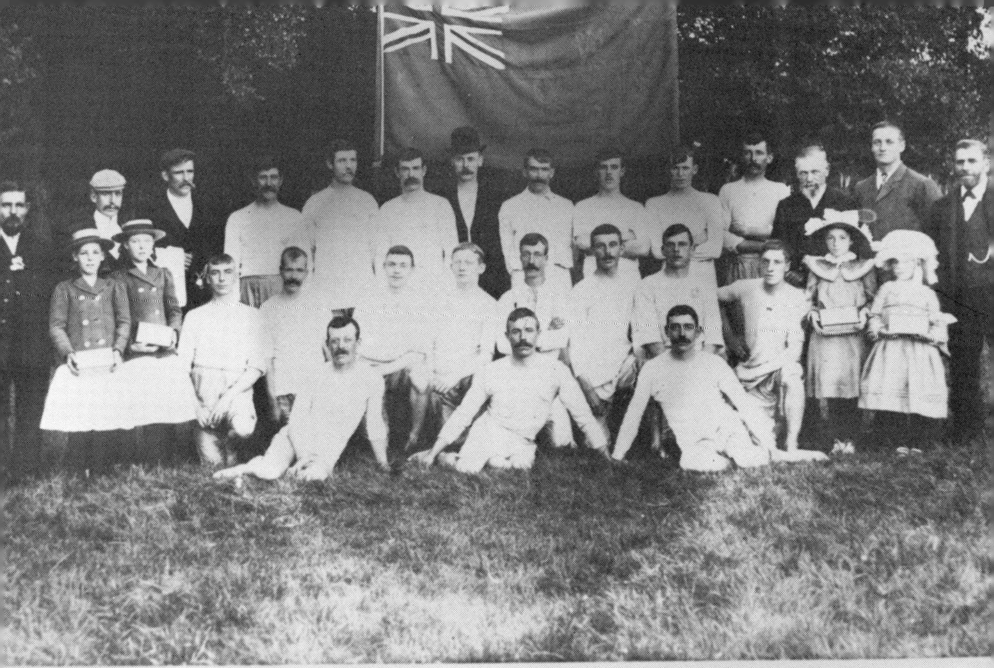

WHITSTABLE GOAL-RUNNING CLUB, 1902-3.

H. Care. W. Parker. W. Care. J. Keam, *Umpire*. J. H. Sargent. J. Rowden. S. Rigden. J. Sargent. W. Keam, *Starter*.

A. Foreman. S. Tottnadine. T. Rigden. J. Keam. J. Smith. O. Laraman. A. Castle. H. Cage.

T. Woolley. A Collar—*Secretary*. R. Court—*Capt*.

WHITSTABLE FOOTBALL CLUB, Season 1908-9.

THANET LEAGUE CHAMPIONS.

Front Row: R. T. Lang, Esq. (President), W. J. Foreman, J. Gambrill, A. Amos, P. Ray, F. Davison, W. Wyver (Hon. Sec.), D. Ward.
Middle Row: H. Tilley, D. C. Keddie, O. Rowden, H. Gambrill, W. Foad, J. Cole, W. Foreman, G. Dunn, F. Humphrey, S. Anderson.
Back Row: H. Keam. W. Barham (Captain) G. Hawkes, R. Gambrell, F. S. Gann.

This photograph of Church Road (now Bridge Approach) at its junction with Church Street was taken c. 1880 and shows the old Butts Cottages, the embankment of the Whitstable–Canterbury railway and the bridge over the main line. On the extreme right in the distance can be seen the two tall chimneys of the coke ovens in the harbour which were built in 1847.

This is how the Gorrell Stream looked before it was covered over in the 1920s. Rising at Millstrood it meandered through the town and entered the sea at the harbour and was tidal before the harbour was excavated in 1830. The original course of the stream was by what is now Fountain Street and entered a small backwater the west side of Cromwell Road and bounded by Harbour Street. This small backwater was quite inadequate so a larger one was built on the opposite side of Cromwell Road. This is now covered over and is a car park and market place. The name Gorrell was originally Gorwell, a very ancient one, and found in documents hundreds of years ago. The photograph shows that part of the Gorrell Stream near Westmeads School looking south-east towards All Saints Church.

Church Street

Gorrell Stream

The Whitstable String Band photographed in the early 1900s. Many prominent tradesmen can be identified in this group.

The Whitstable Town Band photographed in the early 1900s in front of the Bandstand on Tankerton Slopes.

Whitstable String Band

At The Bandstand

The Whitstable Cricket Club photographed at Belmont c. 1875 showing the cemetery on the left (established in 1857) and in the centre distance Downs Farm. This is one of the earliest records of the Whitstable Cricket Club.

This is the earliest known photograph of the Whitstable Football Club taken c. 1883 at the Endowed School in the High Street. Note the lace-up boots and the knee-length 'shorts'. It is believed that Mr. George Kirkby, the headmaster of the Oxford Street Boys School for many years, is the central figure with his foot on the ball.

Whitstable Cricket Club, Belmont

Whitstable Football Club

These quaint little goat chaises plied for hire along Beach Road and Harbour Street for a few coppers. They were started by Harry Cage and continued by Sidney Steer. This photograph taken in 1905 shows a group of these and includes a local policeman anxious to have his photo 'took'.

The 1st Whitstable Scouts (Mrs. Geo. Holdens Own) Band photographed about 1922, possibly at Sholden near Deal. The Scoutmaster Mr. W. R. Blyth, here seen in the centre behind the big drum, is surrounded by four of his sons. E. Austen (on the left of the three at the back) regularly played the 'Last Post' at the War Memorial ceremonies. The Blyth family were also prominent members of the Salvation Army Band.

Goat Chaise at Tankerton

1st Whitstable Scouts Band

Laying the Foundation Stone on 21st October 1925 of the Whitstable and Tankerton Cottage Hospital which really had its beginnings during the First World War when the London Convalescent Hospital was at Cliff Terrace, Marine Parade (now part of the Marine Hotel). After the war a public meeting was held at the Endowed School when it was proposed 'a Cottage Hospital be established at the London Convalescent Hospital'. This was formally opened on 1st April 1919. A year later Mr. Fitt purchased the whole building which then became the Marine Hotel. Another public meeting was held in 1921 when Mr. H. Hudson gave a piece of ground at Pier Avenue towards the new project – The Whitstable and Tankerton Cottage Hospital. The first turf was cut in September 1925 and the foundation stone laid by Lord Northbourne on 21st October 1925. The opening ceremony took place on 8th December 1926 by Col. David Carnegie and was officially named 'The Whitstable and Tankerton Cottage and Convalescent Hospital'.

This photograph shows the Broadway, Swalecliffe and the road widening in progress. The Hardware Stores No. 88 Herne Bay Road is now the Swalecliffe grocers and the Post Office is next door at No. 90, now a fish restaurant. Later on the Post Office made another move, its fourth, to its present site opposite Quinneys Garage. On the opposite side of the road, and out of the picture, was a bungalow later used as a surgery for Doctor Callender and Doctor Glynn. The building is now demolished. The Swalecliffe and Chestfield railway station was opened in 1928 when Mr. Geo Reeves was developing Chestfield.

Laying Foundation Stone,
Whitstable & Tankerton Cottage Hospital

Swalecliffe Broadway

The Oval Skating Rink was a popular recreation for Whitstable people, music was played by an electric organ and a Tudor style restaurant by the side of the rink supplied teas etc. Situated on the Sea Wall, access to the rink was by steps as the rink was some feet below. The land had originally been a timber yard but the great fire of 1869 laid the whole area to waste. Many years later the Whitstable Council endeavoured to buy the land but were unable to get a loan. A private company under the direction of Mr. George Reeves laid the area out as a roller skating rink to be called the 'Oval Skating Rink'. It was opened early in 1914 and continued for a few years. Fairy lights were hung around the rink and fancy dress carnivals were held. In recent years it has become a boat park. The Whitstable Oyster Fleet lies offshore.

Mr. H. Leney working in his forge on the West Beach. Much of his work was making ornamental gates and wrought iron work which was in demand over a wide area. This photograph was taken c. 1950.

The Oval Skating Rink

Mr. Leney's Forge, West Beach

Situated at the top of Borstal Hill the "Long Reach Tavern", here seen on the right of the photograph, was closed in 1934 and moved to the newly built Thanet Way near the Borstal Hill roundabout. The premises shown in the photograph are now a general store. The name 'Long Reach' refers to a yachting phrase i.e. a straight run.

A unique photograph showing an engine and truck of the old Whitstable–Canterbury railway crossing the main line with the newly inaugurated Thanet Belle locomotive underneath. The Thanet Belle was inaugurated on 31st May 1948 but was soon to be overtaken by diesel–electric engines when the line was electrified.

The Long Reach Tavern

Whitstable–Canterbury Railway crossing the Main Line

An early photograph of West Beach showing only seven houses of Wave Crest having been built. There was originally a white stone statue at each end of the front wall but these have long since disappeared. Wave Crest, a row of 18 houses, was built by Thomas Goldfinch.

Men of the Royal Naval Reserve at the Battery, Seasalter, showing the position of the two cannons used for practice firing out to sea. This photograph was taken c. 1880. The Battery today is a holiday camp for the Shaftesbury Society.

West Beach

The Battery, Seasalter

Canterbury Road Milestone

Handing over Whitstable Harbour

Milestones once dotted the road from Canterbury – this one, still in position, though almost covered up, is in the front of No. 50 Canterbury Road and if excavated you would find that it states 6 miles to Canterbury and ½ mile to Whitstable. There is another one, very plain to see, near the top of Clapham Hill and informs us that it is 5 miles to Canterbury and 1½ miles to Whitstable.

Handing-over ceremony of the Whitstable Harbour vested to the Whitstable Urban District Council on 4th January 1958 from British Rail. The harbour was opened on 19th March 1832, a year after the Whitstable–Canterbury railway was constructed, a channel being cut through to the sea on 28th October 1831.

PRICE LIST.

WINES.

PORT.

From the Wood.

	Per doz.
Superior, with body	32s
Fine Old Tawny...	36s

CRUSTED WINES.

Very Old, full flavour	48s
High Class, light...	60s
Vintage Wine, full of wing ...	84s
½-Bottles, very choice	48s
¼-Bottles, well matured... ...	21s
	Per gall.
INVALID PORT	15s. 18s
TARRAGONA	10s

For Children and Invalids.

SHERRY.

	Per doz.
Light, dry	30s
Soft, full	36s
Amontillado	48s
Very Fine Old "Solera" ...	60s
	Per gall.
From the Wood	16s. & 18s

CLARET.

	Per doz.
St. Julien...	24s
Pauillac	36s
St. Estèphe	48s
Léoville	60s

SPECIAL QUOTATIONS FOR VINTAGE WINES

CHAMPAGNE.

	Per doz. bots.	Per 24 ½-bots.
Carte Blanche ...	28s	32s
Louis Reginer White Dry Sillery	60s	65s
Ayala's 1st Quality, 1878	72s	—
Moët's 1st Quality ...	66s	70s
,, White Dry Sillery	66s	70s
Heidsieck Dry Monopole	84s	90s

STILL HOCK.

	Per doz. bots.	Per 24 ½-bots.
Niersteiner	30s	34s
Hockheimer	36s	40s
Geisenheimer ...	42s	46s
Marcobrunner ...	54s	60s

SPARKLING HOCK AND MOSELLE.

	Per doz. bots.	Per 24 ½-bots.
1st Quality ...	54s	58.

SPIRITS.

BRANDY.

	Per doz. Bots.	Gal.
Finest Jersey		16s. & 18s
Good Pale or Brown	42s	21s
Very Fine Old ,,	60s	27s. & 30s
Richot & Co.'s * Pk. label	60s	—
Ditto ** Blue ,,	65s	—
Ditto *** White ,,	70s	—

Hennessy's and Martell's Brandies, three qualities, in Cases, from 60s to 84s.

IRISH & SCOTCH WHISKIES.

	Per doz. bots.	Gall.
Very Fine Old ...	39s & 42s	20s & 21s
Brown & Pank's "10 Blend" Scotch Whisky	54s	—

Sole Agent for Kinahan's L.L., 42s. doz.

RUM.

Fine Old Jamaica ...	30s	15s
Very Fine Old ,, ...	36s	16s 6d

GIN.

Good	28s	—
Finest	32s	13s

FOREIGN AND BRITISH LIQUEURS.

BOTTLED BASS, GUINESS, AND CYDER.

Single Bottles of most of the above can be had at proportionate prices.

Beer Bottles, Casks, Hampers and Cases must be given in exchange or paid for on delivery, the same allowed when they are returned.

An advertisement in Cox's Guide to Whitstable in 1884.
The Good Old Days?

And discount for cash! Did people run up accounts in 1884? Cheapside is the area now occupied by Hatchards in the High Street.

INDEX